As a young schoolboy, Winston Leonard Spencer Churchill showed little promise of the great man he was to become. He was a constant disappointment to his teachers and parents who felt he could have been a far better scholar than he was. He was often criticised for his bad behaviour and untidiness. Despite an unsuccessful career at school, he eventually became a respected journalist, a best selling author and a Nobel prizewinner. Born in 1874, into one of the most famous families in Britain, it was not until the age of sixty-five, when most men are thinking of retirement, that he became the leader of a country at war. The many speeches and broadcasts that he made during the war years are now a part of history. The life story of Churchill tells of the development of the young soldier and politician into the world statesman and the 'father figure' of British politics during the twentieth century.

When he died in 1965, Winston Churchill was given a State Funeral, an honour bestowed on few people outside the Royal Family. He was also given a 21 gun salute, a tribute usually reserved only for the monarch. In this book Eva Bailey tells the story of a remarkable man whose varied careers spanned six reigns.

Eva Bailey is a former teacher and school librarian who has a special interest in history. Her work has been featured on the radio, including BBC Schools Programmes.

Churchill

Eva Bailey

More Wayland History Makers

Adolf Hitler Matthew Holden
Al Capone Mary Letts
Bismarck Richard Kisch
The Borgias David Sweetman
Castro Paul Humphrey
Cecil Rhodes Neil Bates
Cromwell Amanda Purves
Franco Richard Kisch
Goering F. H. Gregory
Jomo Kenyatta Julia Friedman
Joseph Stalin David Hayes and F. H. Gregory
Karl Marx Caroline Seaward
The Last Czar W. H. C. Smith
Lenin Lionel Kochan
Lincoln Philip Clark
Mao Tse Tung Hugh Purcell
Martin Luther King Patricia Baker
Picasso David Sweetman
Rommel F. H. Gregory
Tito Michael Gibson
Washington Philip Clark
The Wright Brothers Russell Ash

First published in 1981 by
Wayland Publishers Limited
49 Lansdowne Place, Hove
East Sussex BN3 1HF.
© Copyright 1981 Wayland Publishers Ltd
ISBN 0 85340 645 6

Printed in the U.K. by
The Pitman Press, Bath

Contents

Prologue

Above Winston Churchill as a boy. He was about seven when this photograph was taken.

Even before Winston Churchill was born, his family held a place in history. His ancestor, John Churchill (1650-1722) was the famous general who successfully commanded the British troops against the French in the battles of Blenheim, Ramillies, Oudenarde and Malplaquet.

John Churchill was created the 1st Duke of Marlborough by William III. Queen Anne rewarded the famous general after his victory at Blenheim in 1704 by building a palace for him — Blenheim Palace at Woodstock near Oxford.

It was in Blenheim Palace on 30th November, 1874 that Winston Leonard Spencer Churchill was born.

The young Churchill did not show any early promise of becoming a great man. He was described as mischievous, restless, red-haired, snubnosed, difficult and the naughtiest boy in the whole world.

His record at school was very poor, but he did eventually gain a deep knowledge of the English language. He had three attempts before he managed to pass the examination to gain entry to Sandhurst, the Royal Military College. It was only as he reached manhood that his qualities and abilities were revealed, and Churchill lost no time in putting them to good use.

Like his ancestor, John Churchill, 1st Duke of Marlborough, Winston Churchill as a man was to gain a place in history.

"I thank you very much for those beautiful presents, those Soldiers and Flags and Castles, they are so nice."
Winston Churchill, aged 7, in a letter to his mother.

Left John Churchill, the first Duke of Marlborough and Winston's ancestor.

His determination and leadership during World War II inspired Britain, and encouraged the Allies to fight for freedom. He also helped to establish the United Nations Organization which was designed to enable the peoples of the world to unite peacefully.

1 Boy into Soldier

Above Lord Randolph Churchill. Winston's father and a notable politician.

Winston Leonard Spencer Churchill was the first child of Lord Randolph Churchill. Winston's mother, formerly Miss Jennie Jerome, was an American, and her father, Leonard Jerome, was a newspaper proprietor.

Lord Randolph was a Member of Parliament. When Winston's grandfather, the 7th Duke of Marlborough, was appointed Lord Lieutenant of Ireland, he took Lord Randolph with him as his private secretary. Winston and his mother also accompanied them, and this was how Winston Churchill came to spend his first five years in Ireland.

The Churchill family was typical of many notable Victorians. Winston's parents were often absent on social or political duties, and he saw little of them. Like many upper-class children of the time, Winston was cared for by a nanny. Her name was Mrs Everest, and she looked after Winston and his younger brother, Jack, who was born in 1880. Mrs Everest stayed with the family for many years, first as a nanny and later as a housekeeper. It was to her that Winston turned when in need, and he always remembered her with affection. Winston was devoted to his mother, but she was always rather a remote figure during his early life.

When Winston was seven years old he was sent to boarding school. Here he found a strict discipline which often amounted to cruelty. Winston was very unhappy, and was sometimes beaten for his lack of

knowledge and mischievous behaviour.

It was Mrs Everest who discovered the signs of ill-treatment. On being informed, Winston's parents immediately transferred him to a school at Brighton. This was run by two ladies named Thomson, and at this school a much kindlier atmosphere existed. Winston stayed until he was thirteen. Here he discovered a delight in reading stories, especially *Treasure Island* and *King Solomon's Mines*. He enjoyed acting and edited a school paper.

Above Winston's mother, the former Jennie Jerome, pictured here with young Winston and his brother Jack.

"She shone for me like the Evening Star. I loved her dearly — but at a distance."
Winston Churchill speaking of his mother.

The only unpleasant episode during this period was when Churchill developed double pneumonia and was very ill. Because it was felt that he was not very strong, it was decided that Winston should not be sent to Eton, where other members of his family had been educated. He was entered for Harrow, the public school situated on a hill.

It was, however, necessary to pass an examination to gain entrance. Winston, who took this examination very seriously, did badly, especially in the Latin paper. However, he was still given a place at the school. At Harrow, his scholastic work was so poor that he always remained in the Lower School. He was unable to understand mathematics and could not comprehend Latin or Greek. It was after he left school that Churchill gained his wide knowledge of the English language. He worked hard to develop this and made great use of it in his speeches and books later in his life.

Churchill had a very good memory. When he was thirteen he won a prize for reciting 1,200 lines from Macauley's *Last Days of Ancient Rome*, without a mistake. Much later in his life he took great pleasure in proving he could still remember these lines.

Swimming was also a favourite pastime. Churchill was also an expert at fencing, and won a silver medal in a school competition. Being an individualist, Winston disliked team games such as cricket or football.

As the time approached when Churchill would leave school, he asked to enter the Army. It was decided he should go to Sandhurst Military College and become an Army Officer. In order to do this, the entrance examination had to be passed. Churchill tried twice, and failed. His father sent him to a 'crammer,' a type of school which specialised in

Left The schoolboy. The boys of Harrow wore top hats, striped trousers and frock coats as their uniform.

intensive study in order to pass examinations. After six months study, Churchill managed to pass the examination, but only just. He gained entry to the cavalry, which was slightly easier than entering the infantry. The demand for places in the cavalry was not so great because few could afford the extra expense of the horses and equipment required. Winston's father, Lord Randolph, was not pleased. He had wished his son to enter the 60th Rifles.

Lord Randolph was a sick man at this time, but he wrote to Winston expressing his disappointment. He criticised his son about his slovenly, happy-go-lucky, harum scarum style of work. Lord Randolph warned Winston that if he didn't stop leading an idle, useless, unprofitable life, he would become a social wastrel and a failure, with a shabby, unhappy, futile existence.

"Personally I am always ready to learn, although I do not always like being taught."
Winston Churchill.

11

The impetuous youth nearly ended not only his career but his life at this time. In the period between leaving school and going to Sandhurst, he stayed for a while at Bournemouth with his aunt, Lady Wimborne. He attempted to jump from a bridge in the garden on to a tree. He missed, and fell thirty feet. He was unconscious for three days and had to remain in bed for three months.

During this time, Winston Churchill became aware of political matters, and began to take an interest in his father's parliamentary career.

When the course at Sandhurst commenced in September 1893, Churchill, at the age of 18, began his training as an army officer.

An amazing change came over him. Freed from the restrictions of a school timetable, Winston Churchill suddenly matured. He enjoyed the life, the open air activities and the challenge of new pursuits. The day at the Military College began at 6.45 a.m. The curriculum included the subjects of military administration and law, map-reading, riding, musketry and tactics. The officer cadets finished their studies at 4 p.m. They were free until the evening, when they gathered for an evening meal. 'Lights out' was at 11 p.m.

Churchill's Sandhurst career was brilliant. Having only just scraped in, by the time he reached the end of the course his name appeared near the top of the Pass List. His best examination subjects were tactics, fortifications and riding.

A month after Churchill completed his course at Sandhurst, on 24th January 1895 his father died. In July, Mrs Everest died also. Churchill had never lost touch with her and always valued her loyalty and affection.

Great changes were taking place in the life of Second Lieutenant Winston Churchill.

Opposite Churchill wearing the uniform of the 4th Hussars. This picture was taken while they were stationed at Bangalore in India.

2 Careers combine

Winston Churchill was posted from Sandhurst to the 4th Hussars, stationed at Aldershot. Here he thoroughly enjoyed the life of an army officer. He was, however, anxious to see active service. During a period of leave from the army he obtained permission to visit Cuba, where Spanish forces were striving to subdue a rebellion, as part of his holiday. Whilst he was there a train he was travelling on was fired upon by the rebel forces. It was Winston's 21st birthday and the first time he had ever experienced being under fire. For his gallant behaviour he was awarded the Spanish military Red Cross.

While he was in Cuba, Churchill sent descriptive letters to the *Daily Graphic*. It was Churchill's first venture into journalism. The letters were published, and Churchill received payment of £5 for each one.

It was about the time that Churchill first began to smoke cigars. In later life he was rarely photographed without his famous cigar.

Winston Churchill returned to England and in 1896 enjoyed the festivities of Queen Victoria's Diamond Jubilee. With his parents he attended numerous social functions and met many of the notable people of the time. He was welcomed into London society, and on one occasion dined with the Prince of Wales, later Edward VII.

Shortly afterwards, Churchill's regiment, the 4th Hussars, was ordered to India. The troops were stationed at Bangalore in South India. Although the

"I found that whatever I might think and argue, I did not hesitate to ask for special protection when about to come under the fire of the enemy, nor to feel sincerely grateful when I got home safe for tea."
Winston Churchill.

Left Polo was one team sport which Churchill enjoyed.

regimental station was situated 923 metres (3,000 ft) above sea level, the climate was hot. There was no fighting in the region: the nearest action was 3,200 kilometres (2,000 miles) away in the northern part of India.

Life was fairly routine at the regimental station. Churchill learned to play polo and he and his fellow officers spent much of their time practising the game. They trained hard in the hope that they would win the Inter-Regimental Cup.

The intense heat necessitated a rest of a few hours in the middle of each day. Winston Churchill often read books during this time. He spent his leisure in a concentrated study of English prose. His choice was wide, and included the works of Macaulay and Darwin. He also read books on history, philosophy and science.

The Churchillian determination began to show. He learned with a thoroughness that was typical when *he* chose to do anything. This reading and learning was put to good use, not only immediately, but throughout his entire life.

Churchill once more became eager to be on active service. He obtained permission from the 4th Hussars to go to the North West Frontier of India, where trouble had broken out. Before he went, he arranged to send reports to the *Daily Telegraph* of London and an Indian newspaper.

Churchill had been transferred to the Malakand Field Force. The hostilities were under way when he arrived and he engaged in some hand to hand fighting. He was awarded a medal and mentioned in dispatches.

Journalistic duties were not neglected. Reports to the papers were sent regularly and were clearly written.

Finding that writing came easily, Churchill wrote a book about the action on the North West Frontier of India. It was based on the material he had reported to the newspapers. The book entitled *The Story of the Malakand Field Force* was published in 1898 and sold well. It earned Churchill an amount equal to two years' pay and, more important, a good reputation as a writer.

The military authorities were, however, annoyed. With the Churchillian bluntness for which he was later to become famous, the author had openly criticised their faults and mistakes.

After Malakand, Churchill returned to his regiment at the base in Southern India. He continued writing and produced his only novel, *Savrola*. This book was strangely prophetic as many of the incidents described in the book were similar to events later in Churchill's own life. An example of this is a description of a battle fleet storming its way through a narrow strait which bears close resemblance to Churchill's plans for Gallipoli. When the book was published, there were a number of kind reviews in newspapers, but none of them considered *Savrola* to be a masterpiece.

During this period, Churchill did not forget that he was a soldier. Wherever there was likely to be a battle, he longed to be there. At about this time trouble had begun to develop in the Sudan. Britain was planning to drive south down the Nile to retake the Sudan which had been lost thirteen years earlier. General Sir Herbert Kitchener was in charge. Not without difficulty — for he had offended those in command by his outspoken comments in his writing — Churchill managed to become attached to the 21st Lancers. The condition was that he paid his own expenses. In order to earn the money, he again contracted to send reports

"I work all day and every day at the book . . . It ought to be good since it is the best I can do."
Churchill, writing to his mother about "The River War," December 1898.

"Solitary trees, if they grow at all, grow strong, and a boy deprived of a father's care often develops, if he escapes the perils of youth, an independence and vigour of thought which may restore in after life the the heavy loss of early days."
Churchill, 'The River War.'

from the front, this time for the *Morning Post* at a fee of £15 per column.

Churchill arrived at the front in time to take part in the battle of Omdurman in September 1898. One of the last great cavalry charges, where the opposing forces faced each other and then attacked, took place during this battle. The charge was undertaken by the 21st Lancers. The British won, but sustained a great number of casualties. Winston Churchill was in some of the fiercest fighting, but came through safely.

It was the end of an era. Modern warfare, with machine guns and mechanised equipment was, in future, to replace the horse.

For the second time, Churchill recorded his experiences in a book. It was entitled *"The River War"* and comprised two volumes describing the Sudan campaign and Britain's earlier relations with the area. This book, with its vivid descriptions, was even more successful than *The Story of the Malakand Field Force*.

Churchill returned to his regiment now in North India. By this time he felt he needed a wider life. Having established himself as an author and journalist, he decided to make writing his career and also to take a greater interest in politics. He resigned his army commission, having been a soldier for four years.

3 Prisoner and politician

Although Winston had never been very close to his father, he often thought about his political career. Before joining the Army, Winston had met numerous politicians at his home. He was always keen to discuss matters with them, and never lost an opportunity to express his own views.

While in the Army, Winston considered the possibility of politics becoming his future career.

During one of his periods of leave, Churchill approached the Conservative Central Office in London and asked to be allowed to make a political speech at a meeting. Churchill had some doubts as to whether he would be able to do this. One difficulty was a slight speech impediment which made him unable to pronounce the letter "s" correctly. He also realised that making a public speech was a very different matter from preparing a written report. Churchill was given his opportunity and addressed a meeting at a garden party in Bath. All went well. He made a good impression.

After resigning from the Army, Churchill was approached by the Conservative party and asked to fight a by-election. On 20th June 1899, Winston Leonard Spencer Churchill was adopted as the Conservative candidate for Oldham, and began his campaign. He spoke at many meetings, sometimes as many as three or four in one evening, and addressed packed audiences.

Voting took place and the result was declared on 6th

"I thought he was a young man of promise, but it appears he was a young man of promises."
A. J. Balfour, speaking of Churchill in 1899.

Right Churchill in the uniform of the South African Light Horse regiment.

July. Churchill had been defeated by the Liberal candidate, Walter Runciman. The defeat did not dishearten Churchill.

At this time there was considerable unrest in South Africa. Britain had ruled the Colony of South Africa since 1815. Trouble with the African natives, the Zulus, had been subdued, but the Boers (Dutch farmers who had settled in South Africa nearly two centuries earlier) now wanted to govern South Africa independently.

The South African War, the second war against the Boers, broke out in 1899, only a few months after Churchill's parliamentary defeat.

Churchill needed paid employment. His reputation as a journalist was high, and the *Morning Post* offered him £250 a month to be their civilian war correspondent. Churchill agreed, and in October set sail for South Africa.

On 15th November 1899, when he had only been in South Africa for a fortnight, Churchill was invited to travel on an armoured train and inspect the position of the enemy in the troubled area.

The journey was never completed. The train was derailed and then ambushed by a party of Boers. Churchill offered his services, and while the officer in charge supervised troops who were defending the wrecked train, Churchill took charge of operations to clear the line. Churchill became separated from the main party and was taken prisoner by a horseman. Later he discovered that many others had also been captured.

Churchill was sent to the prisoner-of-war camp at the State Schools Prison, Pretoria. He became very frustrated with the restrictions of prison life and planned to escape. Four weeks after being captured, he succeeded.

Above This picture was taken shortly after Winston's escape from the prisoner of war camp at Pretoria.

Friendly territory was 483 kms (300 miles) away. Churchill wisely kept under cover by day. One night he travelled in a goods train, hiding himself among coal sacks. Another night he was forced to walk, as no trains were running. Since he had neither compass nor map, he had to follow the railway track in order to keep any sense of direction.

The Boers offered a reward of £25 for the capture of Churchill, dead or alive.

Six days after his escape, Churchill managed to board a train and cross the frontier into Portuguese East Africa. He was weak from his experience and he had lost a lot of weight, but he was free.

The news of Churchill's escape was received at home with jubilation, for it came at a time when England was having little success in the South African War.

Churchill did not return home immediately. He attached himself to the South African Light Horse, a regiment nicknamed 'Cockyoli Birds,' and continued to send reports to the *Morning Post*. He was among the first to enter Pretoria with the victorious army after the fall of the city. He then returned to England.

Churchill had now established his reputation as an author and journalist, and had also become a national hero.

A general election was to be held in October 1900. While his popularity and reputation were high, Churchill decided to contest the election. He again accepted the nomination for the seat at Oldham. At the election, Churchill defeated Walter Runciman, gaining a majority of 222 votes.

At the age of twenty-five, Winston Churchill was a Member of Parliament in what proved to be the last election of Queen Victoria's reign. The Queen died on 23rd January 1901.

King Edward VII opened the new Parliament on February 14th, and Winston Churchill took his seat in the House of Commons. It was the beginning of a new reign and the beginning of the most important part of Churchill's career.

Churchill made his maiden speech (his first speech) to Parliament on 18th February. Just as he had offended his army superiors by his criticisms of them in his books, some of his fellow Members of Parliament were annoyed by his frankness, and especially by what he said regarding the South African War.

In his closing words, he paid tribute to his late father, Lord Randolph Churchill. Lord Randolph had been a noted politician and held office as the Chancellor of the Exchequer. Young Winston Churchill, as he took his seat in the back benches, seemed to be continuing where his father had left off.

But, as time went on, it became clear that there was at least one vital matter on which he could not agree with his political party, the Conservatives.

The Minister for the Colonies, Joseph Chamberlain, was determined to abandon Free Trade and pressed for tariff reform, whereby a tariff (or tax) was to be put on foreign goods coming into the country. Churchill staunchly defended Free Trade — so much so that members of his own party became hostile towards him. In 1904, after three and a half years as a Member of Parliament, Winston Churchill left the Conservatives and joined the Liberals. From now on Churchill made rapid progress in his parliamentary career. At the 1906 General Election, the Liberal Party won easily and Churchill was made Secretary of State for the Colonies. It was his first official post. In 1908, he joined the Cabinet (the Council of Ministers responsible for the government)

Above The rising young politician. This picture was taken in 1904 when Churchill had joined the Liberal Party.

Right Winston Churchill and Lloyd George were close personal friends.

as President of the Board of Trade. A year later, Churchill became a Privy Councillor, one of the body which advises the King on matters of state.

As usual, Churchill gave all his energies to whatever he undertook. He pressed for the introduction of social services and social security. At a time when men worked long hours for low wages, Churchill urged an eight hour day at the coal face. He introduced laws forbidding the employment of boys under fourteen years of age in coal mines. Churchill also played a part in bringing in the first National Insurance Scheme. A friendship sprang up between Winston Churchill and David Lloyd George, a future Prime Minister. Churchill supported many of Lloyd George's ideas, although he went his own individual way. Churchill believed he had a personal destiny, and that his own political achievement was a part of it.

4 World War I

In 1908, Winston Churchill married Clementine Hozier, the daughter of an Army Officer. She proved to be his strong supporter, always ready to help in the difficulties and responsibilities he encountered.

In 1910, Churchill became the Home Secretary. In November of that year, unrest among the workers became apparent. A miners' strike in South Wales

"In September, 1908, I married and lived happily ever after."
Churchill.

Below Winston Churchill and his wife Clementine at the time of their marriage.

Above Churchill in his role as Home Secretary attends the siege of the house in Sidney Street.

"Europe is trembling on the verge of a general war, the Austrian ultimatum to Serbia being the most insolent document of its kind ever devised."
Churchill, writing to his wife just before the outbreak of World War One.

reached serious proportions and riots took place in the Rhondda Valley. In the town of Tonypandy, shops were wrecked. The County police, strengthened by reinforcements from the Metropolitan police, restored law and order.

Troops were sent to the area, but, on instructions from Winston Churchill, these were held in reserve. It was a wise decision, as the police were able to control the area and army action was not necessary.

The following year, 1911, Churchill's love of being to the forefront of any action again showed itself. Two men, thought to be anarchists, barricaded themselves in a building in London's East End. Churchill ordered troops to assist the police. Then Churchill himself turned up to watch operations at what became known as 'The Siege of Sidney Street.' The siege ended and the gunmen died when the building they were in caught fire.

In October 1911, Churchill was made First Lord of the Admiralty. This appointment was of crucial importance, both to Churchill and to the country.

He now devoted his time and energy to improving an already strong Navy. In the same way as he had pressed for better conditions for the working man, he improved sailors' pay and proposed better leisure facilities.

The battle fleet was strengthened, and oil replaced coal as the chief fuel.

Winston Churchill formed the Royal Naval Flying Corps and even learned to fly himself. At this time, too, he fostered what was to become the modern tank. The original unwieldy contraption on caterpillar tracks was nicknamed "Winston's Folly."

Churchill paid close attention to events on the Continent. An assassination at Sarajevo, the capital of Bosnia, on 28th June 1914, caused unrest in the whole

of Europe. Bosnia had been annexed by Austria-Hungary, and this was resented by Russia. Archduke Franz Ferdinand, heir to the Austro-Hungarian throne, was shot dead as he travelled in his car after being received by the Mayor of Sarajevo at the Town Hall.

This action increased the likelihood of war between Russia and Austria-Hungary. Each had allies in Europe. Russia was supported by Serbia, and France was bound by her allegiance to Russia to join with them. Opposing these countries were Austria-Hungary and Germany.

In Britain, a Grand Review of the fleet was held at Spithead in July 1914. Instead of allowing the ships to disperse after the Review, Churchill ordered them to take up their battle stations in the North Sea.

Above Churchill was a popular figure with the Royal Navy. Here he is inspecting a guard of honour on a visit to the Fleet.

The tension in Europe increased, and soon a major
war — World War I — had commenced. England
entered into the conflict when Germany, in order to
wage war on France, sent troops into Belgium,
although Belgium was neutral.

War was declared on August 4th, 1914. The British
Fleet, under the control of Winston Churchill, was
ready.

Churchill dashed everywhere. Soon after hostilities
commenced, he visited Dunkirk in France to
supervise air operations. The German advance
continued, and the Belgian government decided to
abandon Antwerp. Churchill immediately went to
Antwerp. He persuaded the Belgians to continue to
hold out, and even took charge of the defence
operations for three days. It was unfortunate that,
after Churchill left, the Belgian government decided
to give up the struggle.

The British Navy, fully equipped and trained as a

**"There is one thing they cannot
take from you: the Fleet was ready."**
*Lord Kitchener to Churchill, after
the failure of the Dardanelles
Campaign.*

result of Churchill's forethought, had spectacular success. It sank the German Pacific fleet off the Falkland Islands.

But the Germans shelled Scarborough and Hartlepool on the English east coast in daylight. Churchill was severely criticised for allowing this to happen. He was held responsible for the defence of coastal areas, comparing the ability of the bulldog (a symbol of Britain) with the determination of the Navy to defeat the enemy.

The war was not going well for England and her allies. Churchill and his naval advisers prepared a scheme to surprise the enemy. Instead of attacking only on the European battlefront, they planned to attack through the Eastern Mediterranean countries — through the enemy's back door.

The government agreed that a naval attack should be made in order to seize the Dardanelles from Turkey. These important straits protected the city of Constantinople. If they were controlled by the British it would also assist the advance of the Russian Army. Churchill insisted that a military force would be needed on land to follow up the naval attack. The use of troops in the action was not approved, although, reluctantly, a small number of military personnel were eventually sent. At this time combined operations by land and sea were not a normal wartime policy. Churchill, with reasoning ahead of his time, could see the necessity for a combined operation.

The British Navy attacked on 18th March 1915. The operation was not easy. The ships had difficulty in sailing through the minefields, and met more opposition from the Turks than had been expected.

A week later, troops (which were not under Churchill's authority) were sent. They landed on the Gallipoli peninsula, but the soldiers were unable to make progress.

"The nose of the bulldog has been slanted backwards, so that he can breathe without letting go."
Churchill, 1914.

"This is no ordinary war, but a struggle between nations for life and death. It raises passions between nations of the most terrible kind. It effaces the old landmarks and frontiers of our civilisation."
Churchill, in The Times, November 1st, 1914.

Above During his lifetime, Churchill made many speeches. This was despite a slight speech impediment.

"The maxim of the British people is 'Business as usual'."
Churchill, speaking at the Guildhall, London, November 9th, 1914.

"War is a game with a good deal of chance in it, and, from the little I have seen of it, I should say that nothing in war ever goes right, except by accident."
Churchill.

The operation was a failure. Rather unfairly Churchill was blamed for this catastrophe. He argued that the blunder occurred because he did not have complete authority over the whole operation. It was not known at the time, but had the British bombardment continued for only a few more hours the enemy defences would have collapsed, as their ammunition was running out.

In May 1915, a coalition government was formed between the Liberals and the Conservatives. Coalition meant that the political parties agreed not to press their differing views, but to work together for the good of the country. Winston Churchill was removed from office as the First Lord of the Admiralty. Churchill was in disgrace. It was the worst set-back in his career.

The Prime Minister appointed him to the government as the Chancellor of the Duchy of Lancaster. This appointment, which had no political power, did not suit the active-minded Churchill. He resigned his seat as Member of Parliament in November 1915.

Churchill again joined the Army, and on 4th

January 1916 he became the Lieutenant Colonel commanding the 6th Royal Scots Fusiliers. He was posted to Europe, and spent six months of his service in the trenches in France. In the trenches — very deeply dug ditches in the earth — soldiers sought protection from enemy fire.

Meanwhile changes were taking place within the Coalition Government, and on 7th December 1916, Lloyd George became the Prime Minister instead of Mr. Asquith. Although some M.P.'s still opposed Churchill, Lloyd George insisted on including him in the Government. Eight months after taking up his army appointment, Winston Churchill returned to Parliament as the Minister for Munitions.

A Commission of Inquiry was held into the Dardanelles Campaign, and Churchill was officially cleared of any responsibility for the disaster.

As Minister of Munitions, Churchill supervised the production of guns, aeroplanes, ammunition and tanks. He inspected the factories and visited the workers, urging them to greater effort.

Churchill arranged for the production of tanks called 'Big Willies'. Three hundred and seventy-eight were used in an attack at Cambrai in France on 20th November 1917. The result was a decisive victory. The Royal Commission recorded the fact that it was due to the receptivity, courage and driving force of Winston Spencer Churchill that the tank came into being.

World War I ended on 11th November 1918. Churchill's career during hostilities had wavered between success and failure. But as the war finished Churchill was once again in favour.

Above and below During the First World War, Churchill toured the country rallying workers in factories to meet the demands made by the war.

5 Between the wars

After World War I, Churchill tackled many problems, including the re-settlement of troops into civilian life. His parliamentary career progressed and in 1921 he became Colonial Secretary.

The war-time Coalition Government ended in 1922. Lloyd George was defeated in the Election and Bonar Law became the Conservative Prime Minister. Winston Churchill also lost his Parliamentary Seat and was unsuccessful at two by-elections he contested. He was recovering from appendicitis when he should have been fighting the election of 1922. It was now twenty-two years since he had first been elected a Member of Parliament.

Since he no longer held a political appointment, he again turned to writing. The result was *A World Crisis*, a six volume account of World War One. Financially, it was a success. Churchill also inherited a large sum of money, and bought Chartwell, a large country house near Westerham, Kent. At his newly acquired home, Churchill built walls and tiled roofs. He was invited to become a member of the Amalgamated Union of Building Trades Workers and joined as a bricklayer.

He also painted as a hobby. He liked to use oils, and painted landscapes and flowers rather than portraits.

Churchill successfully regained a seat in Parliament in the General Election of October 1924. For some time he had felt that the Liberal Party, to which he belonged, did not form an effective

"In the twinkling of an eye, I found myself without an office, without a seat, without a party and without an appendix."
Churchill, on losing his seat in the 1922 General Election, at which time he was recovering from an operation for appendicitis.

"Anyone can rat, but I flatter myself that it takes a certain amount of ingenuity to re-rat."
Churchill, on returning to the Conservative Party in 1924.

Left When not involved in politics, Churchill often relaxed by building walls and houses.

Above Churchill leaves Number 11 Downing Street, the official residence of the Chancellor, to give his budget speech to the Commons in 1925.

opposition to the Labour and Communist Parties, with whose policies he disagreed. He felt that the Conservative party was fulfilling this need, and so, once again, he became a Conservative.

The Conservatives held the majority of seats in this Parliament and Stanley Baldwin was the Prime Minister. He made Winston Churchill the Chancellor of the Exchequer.

Churchill was a fine war leader, but he was not a financial expert. The Chancellor of the Exchequer in the previous Labour Government had recommended a return to the Gold Standard. This meant that it should be possible for every one pound note to be exchanged for its value in gold. Accepting advice from the Bank of England and also from his own advisers, Churchill put the pound back on the Gold Standard. Unfortunately, the value of the pound was placed too high, and this made it difficult for British traders to sell goods to foreign countries.

British coal in particular was priced out of world markets. Mine owners and other employers tried to remedy the matter by cutting wages. Industrial unrest soon spread.

Many favoured Churchill's policy, but John Maynard Keynes, a Cambridge economist, wrote a pamphlet called *The Economic Consequences of Mr. Churchill*. Keynes warned that Churchill's measures as Chancellor of the Exchequer were creating unemployment and would lead to industrial troubles.

They did, and in May 1926 resulted in a General Strike in which many Trade Unions called on their men to stop work. Starting on 6th May, the strike lasted nine days, although mine workers stayed out for six months.

There were no newspapers, and Stanley Baldwin,

the Prime Minister, made Churchill responsible for producing an official emergency newspaper, the *British Gazette*. It was printed on the *Morning Post* presses and gave important items of news. With his usual energy and determination, Winston Churchill produced his paper with the help of volunteers. The eighth issue, on the last day of the strike, had a circulation of over two million.

As Chancellor of the Exchequer, Churchill introduced a number of measures which were

"Some men change their party for the sake of their principles; others their principles for the sake of their party."
Winston Churchill.

Below Two contrasting views of the General Strike as seen by the Press.

Right Chamberlain returns from Munich. It was hoped that the Munich Agreement would prevent a war with Hitler's Germany.

welcomed. He improved the pension position of the aged, widows and orphans, and reduced income tax.

At the General Election in 1929, the Labour party gained a victory, and although Churchill retained his Conservative seat, he was a member of the Opposition.

The Labour Party won by only a small majority, and in 1931 a National Government, composed of members of all parties, was elected to deal with the economic crisis. In this year the Gold Standard was finally abandoned.

Churchill's political activities at this time were not spectacular, although he often made his views known. He disagreed with Conservative policy which aimed at giving India some degree of self government. He believed that the British Empire should always be preserved and considered that India was not ready or able to govern itself. After many years of struggle, the India Bill was passed in 1935. This gave India the status of a Dominion. Churchill accepted the situation with reluctance.

Churchill wrote one of his most important works during this period. It was a biography of his ancestor, the first Duke of Marlborough. The four volumes, entitled *Marlborough, his Life and Times* were published between 1933-8.

In these years, when Churchill seemed to be a shadowy figure in the background of politics, he still held his own opinions and voiced them, believing that Germany's rising power was a danger. When the Prime Minister, Neville Chamberlain, signed the Munich Agreement in September 1938, it was welcomed by some as 'peace with honour.' But Churchill warned that this was not the case. He called the Munich Agreement 'a defeat without a War.' He could sense the rumblings of conflict.

6 World War II — Prime Minister

In the early 1930's, the increasing strength of the German National Socialist Workers' Party caused Churchill to become concerned. Few people seemed to share his alarm regarding the activities of the Nazi party, as it was called, but Churchill realised the ruthlessness of the leader, Adolf Hitler.

On 30th January, 1933, Hitler became the Chancellor of the German state, the Reich. As Churchill had warned, Germany began to re-arm and make large quantities of military equipment.

Under Hitler's leadership, the German forces soon began to occupy the Rhineland, the Ruhr and Saar coalfields, Austria and the Sudeten lands bordering the northern and western borders of Czechoslovakia.

It was when Hitler's forces were placed along the Czechoslovakian border in September 1938, that the British Prime Minister, Neville Chamberlain, went to Munich in Germany in an attempt to prevent war. Mr. Chamberlain conferred with Adolf Hitler, Mussolini of Italy, and Daladier of France. They all signed the Munich Agreement.

In this document, Hitler promised not to overstep the boundaries of other countries, but Winston Churchill did not believe Hitler would keep his word. Churchill was right, and the Munich Agreement was broken in March 1939, when Hitler claimed control of the whole of Czechoslovakia.

Hitler marched on, and when his troops entered Poland on 1st September, 1939, war became a certainty. Two days later, on 3rd September, 1939, England and France issued a declaration of war on Germany.

The British Government was re-organised, and immediately Churchill was given the Cabinet post of First Lord of the Admiralty. Although he was almost sixty-five years of age, he undertook his duties with keenness and vigour.

The Navy went into action without delay, and within a few months was responsible for the sinking of the German battleship, *The Graf Spee*. In February 1940, the Navy rescued 299 captive British naval personnel from *the Altmark,* a German prison ship.

Neither the Army nor the Air Force was called on to undertake any significant missions at this time. People referred to the 'phoney war'. Only the Navy, under the direction of Churchill, went into action.

But the German Army soon became active. Churchill sensed that there was a danger to Norway. He wanted the Norwegian coast to be mined as a precautionary measure. Other ministers did not share his urgent concern, and were afraid to violate Norwegian neutrality. Churchill persisted, and in April 1940 the plan was approved. It was too late, for in April 1940 Germany occupied Norway and Denmark. The combined forces of the British Royal Navy and Royal Air Force made an attempt to assist the Norwegians in a struggle to overcome the German invader. Like the Dardanelles Campaign in World War I, the operation was a failure.

With the collapse of Norway, the statesmen of the British Government finally lost confidence in the Prime Minister, Neville Chamberlain. The Members of Parliament felt that he was not taking sufficiently strong action to curb Hitler's onslaught. Chamber-

Above Churchill always argued that a strong Navy was Britain's best defence.

Above Throughout the war years Churchill's gruff voice and determined speeches encouraged a civilian population suffering from bombing raids, rationing and food shortages.

lain was asked to give up his office as Prime Minister, and his Government forced to resign.

On 10th May 1940, King George VI sent for Churchill and asked him to form a Government. It was the beginning of the most distinguished phase of Churchill's career, that of war-time Prime Minister. On the same day, 10th May, Holland and Belgium were invaded by Hitler.

The Government Churchill formed was a coalition representing all political parties. It was led by five cabinet minsters. Churchill included himself in this number, and in addition to being Prime Minister, held the office of Minister of Defence.

The position in Europe was desperate. Four days after Churchill took office, Holland collapsed under the pressure of the German attack, and only a fortnight later, Belgian resistance gave way.

Churchill made a total of four visits to France and had discussions with the French leaders regarding the

"**I felt as if I were walking with Destiny, and that all my past life had been but a preparation for this hour and for this trial.**"
Churchill, on becoming Prime Minister.

conduct and progress of the war. For some time, Churchill had confidence in the strength of the French Army, but the ruthless German advance split the French and British Forces and the Germans captured the French towns of Calais and Boulogne.

In June 1940, the British Army was pushed westwards and trapped in the Dunkirk region of the French coast. It was at this time that the French surrendered.

Churchill remained strong and determined. He addressed the House of Commons with a speech which was a rallying cry to the whole nation. And the nation responded. Six hundred and fifty little ships gallantly crossed the English Channel under the protection of the Navy. This motley armada included small ships and tiny pleasure boats never intended to cross the Channel. They were not crewed by Royal Navy personnel, but by their owners and other volunteers. They rescued 233,000 British and 112,000

"We shall not flag or fail. We shall go on to the end; we shall fight in France, we shall fight on the seas and oceans, we shall fight with growing confidence and growing strength in the air, we shall defend our island, whatever the cost may be; we shall fight on the beaches, we shall fight on the landing grounds, we shall fight in the fields and in the streets, we shall fight in the hills; we shall never surrender."
Churchill addressing the House of Commons, June 4th, 1940, after the Dunkirk evacuation.

Below Wherever he visited, Churchill was always assured of a warm welcome from the troops and civilians.

"The British Empire and its Commonwealth last for a thousand years, men will still say 'This was their finest hour.' "
Churchill, broadcasting on June 18th, 1940.

French soldiers from the Dunkirk beaches and brought them back to England. 'Dunkirk is not a defeat' said Churchill, 'it is a wonderful challenge.' The British Army lived to fight again.

While the Navy was relatively strong, the Royal Air Force was very short of planes and pilots. Four hundred and thirty British aircraft had been lost in the few weeks before the Dunkirk evacuation, in the desperate attempt to save France from the invading Germans. Now that France had fallen and England was on her own, the manufacture of fighter and bomber aircraft was speeded up. Every attempt was made to repair damaged aircraft as quickly as possible and to keep all planes airworthy. The Royal Air Force needed more pilots. The training schedule was revised so that pilots were trained more quickly. In August 1940, the Royal Air Force had 700 fighters — but the Luftwaffe, the German Air Force, had 3,500 aircraft.

Churchill was aware that help was badly needed, and his thoughts and actions were not only on one battle-front. He negotiated with the United States and asked if Britain could have the use of fifty American destroyers. This request was granted. Next, the Lease-Lend Act came into being. Under this, arrangements were made for Britain to receive war supplies from America immediately, and pay for them at a later date.

Churchill knew that the conquered French fleet, now berthed at Oran, a North African port, was likely to be used by the Germans in an invasion of England. On Churchill's instructions, British naval aircraft were used to bombard the French fleet and put it out of action.

In Britain, many of the men not serving in the armed forces formed themselves into a civilian army. At first this was called the L.D.V., (Local Defence Volunteers), later it was re-named the Home Guard.

Churchill realised what would happen next. 'The Battle of France is over,' he said. 'I expect that the Battle of Britain is about to begin.' With Churchill as leader, England was ready to face a German invasion.

Above The Home Guard was made up of men who through age, illness or occupation were unable to join the regular forces.

"If we open a quarrel between the past and the present, we shall find we have lost the future."
Churchill, addressing the House of Commons, June 18th, 1940.

7 World War II — Britain under fire

Churchill clearly stated his war aim. It was 'Victory — victory at all costs'.

It was known that Germany intended to invade England. Invading forces had not succeeded in Britain since William the Conqueror and his armies had disembarked at Hastings in 1066. In 1940, the British Navy was the strongest form of defence, although the greatest danger of German invasion came from the air. The German Air Force, the Luftwaffe, made attacks on British naval vessels and merchant shipping in the English Channel. England had the advantage of a new invention — Radar. This gave an early warning of the approach of enemy aircraft and enabled British fighter planes to intercept the enemy aircraft before the target was reached. Many Radar stations, with their huge masts, were situated along the English south coast.

Hitler then turned his attention to the Radar Stations, and the German Air Force attempted to eliminate them. Many were put out of action.

Churchill was aware of the seriousness of the situation, but he was strong in his leadership of the country. He inspired the members of the armed forces and the civilians with a determination to overcome the enemy.

Hitler extended his attack on England. In the middle of August 1940, large formations of German bombers, protected by Messerschmitt fighter planes, flew to England in an attempt to put English ports,

"The second phase of the campaign is over with the capture of Paris. The third phase had begun. It is the pursuit and final destruction of the enemy."
Hitler, June 14th, 1940.

"Death and sorrow will be the companions of our journey; hardship our garment, constancy and valour our only shield. We must be united, we must be undaunted, we must be inflexible."
Churchill reporting on the war situation to the House of Commons, October 8th, 1940.

Left The famous V for Victory sign which was associated with Churchill and became the symbol of British determination to win the war.

airfields and factories out of action. The planes were intercepted by Spitfire and Hurricane fighters from the Royal Air Force. Many enemy aircraft were prevented from reaching their targets.

Churchill followed the progress of the war in the air closely, and visited the Operations Room of the Royal

Air Force. On one occasion, as he watched the board on which a fierce air battle was being plotted, Churchill enquired, 'What reserves have we?' He received the sombre reply, 'There are none.'

The same Royal Air Force pilots flew to intercept the Luftwaffe as many as six times a day. In fighting the Battle of Britain to defend the people of England, they had little time for rest and re-fuelling. On 20th August 1940, Churchill paid tribute to the airmen in a statement which was to become famous: 'Never in the field of human conflict was so much owed by so many to so few.'

There were losses of both British and German planes and pilots, but Hitler was unable to conquer

"We shall defend every village, every town and every city. The vast mass of London itself, fought street by street, could easily devour an entire hostile army; and we would rather see London laid in ruins and ashes than that it should be tamely and abjectly enslaved."
Churchill broadcasting on July 14th, 1940.

Below An operations room. Information was passed to the girls through their headphones and they then plotted the numbers and positions of the aircraft on the large map in front of them.

Above Pilots such as these young men flew many missions a day.

England by defeating the Royal Air Force. By mistake one German bomber dropped a number of bombs on London. Immediately Churchill ordered the Royal Air Force to bomb Berlin, and in return Hitler instructed the Luftwaffe to carry out bombing raids on other British cities.

As the German raids took place, there was much damage and many casualties, especially in London.

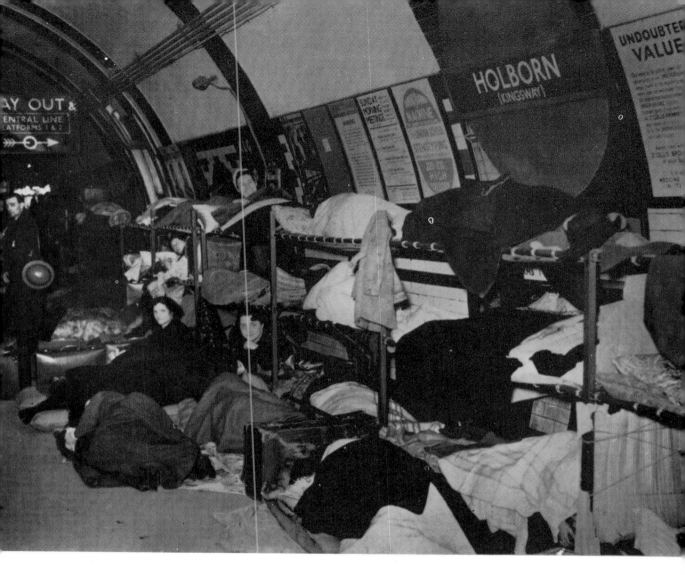

In order to escape from the bombing, when the warning siren sounded people took refuge in specially built air raid shelters. Many Londoners sought safety below street level on the platforms of the London Underground Stations.

Churchill had a War Room which was built well below ground level and this was both his office and bedroom. He broadcast to the nation from this room

Above During the nightly bombing raids on London many people sought shelter in the Underground stations.

on several occasions during the war. In his radio broadcast on 11th September 1940, Churchill warned the nation of the likelihood of invasion. Although he spoke of new perils, he also boosted the morale of the people and strengthened their determination to overcome all difficulties in order to defeat the enemy.

Churchill worked with boundless energy. In addition to attending meetings and making major decisions regarding the conduct of the war, he made extensive tours of bombed areas, airfields, military camps and factories. He was a welcome and respected figure wherever he went.

Winston Churchill concerned himself with world-wide matters. He master-minded the Atlantic Charter and discussed this with Roosevelt, the United States President, aboard HMS *Prince of Wales* in Argentia

Above Mr and Mrs Churchill inspect the damage caused to some houses during a raid on London.

Opposite Children were often evacuated to country areas. Those that stayed on in the towns often had to practise wearing their gas masks, as in this picture.

"This wicked man Hitler, the repository and embodiment of many forms of soul-destroying hatred, this monstrous product of former wrongs and shame."
Churchill broadcasting on September 11th, 1940.

51

Above Churchill arrives at
Downing Street having been told of
the Japanese attack on Pearl
Harbour.

"The German Armed Forces must
be prepared to crush Soviet Russia
in a quick campaign before the end
of the war against England."
Hitler, December 18th, 1940.

Bay, Newfoundland, in August 1941. The Atlantic
Charter set out four fundamental freedoms — freedom of speech, freedom of worship, freedom from
want and freedom from fear. These were to be the
peace-time aims following the war.

The war was spreading on many fronts. In June
1941, Hitler attacked Russia. Although Churchill
greatly opposed Russia's Communist policies, he
knew that all countries must work together to
overcome Hitler. Churchill conferred with the
Russian leaders Stalin and Molotov, and promised to
give Russia whatever help was possible.

The Japanese had been invading China for a
number of years. Suddenly, in December 1941, they
attacked the American Naval Base at Pearl Harbour in
the Pacific Ocean. Until now, the American policy
had been to supply England with war weapons but
not to enter the war. The position changed immediately. America came into the war, and the co-
operation between Churchill and the American
President became even closer.

The war continued to creep into other areas. Hitler
had sent his Afrika Korps, of which he was particularly proud, to North Africa in January 1941. At
first the German forces were defeated, and the British
8th Army, nicknamed the Desert Rats, captured
Tobruk. But the battle in North Africa went on, with
opposing forces alternately meeting success and
failure. Eventually, in June 1942, Tobruk was re-
captured by the Germans and the Desert Rats had to
retreat to El Alamein. Churchill and his ministers
decided that it was vital for the British and Allied
Forces to conquer French North Africa in order to
curb Hitler and his Italian ally, Mussolini. Churchill
made General Alexander the Commander-in-Chief of
the Middle East, and in August gave General Mont-

gomery command of the Eighth Army.

It was not until the autumn of 1942 that Churchill's strategies began to be effective. Montgomery gained a decisive victory at El Alamein in North Africa, and this proved to be the turning point of the war.

The Americans landed with the British troops in Algeria, Morocco and Tunisia. In Spring 1943, General Alexander reported to Churchill that the enemy had been cleared from most of the Middle East countries.

Churchill now began the attack on North West Europe. It was code-named 'Operation Overlord'. Just as in World War I, Churchill had encouraged the development of the tank, he now promoted such

Above Churchill had great faith in the abilities of General Montgomery. This faith was justified when the Eighth Army were victorious at El Alamein.

"Before Alamein we never had a victory. After Alamein we never had a defeat."
Churchill in his 'War Memoirs'.

Above Troopships cross the Channel to storm the Normandy beaches on D-Day.

"This is not the end. It is not even the beginning of the end. But it is, perhaps, the end of the beginning." *Churchill, referring to the Battle of Egypt, in a speech at the Mansion House, London, November 10th, 1942.*

Opposite VE (Victory in Europe) Day. Mr Churchill makes his victory speech from a balcony while hundreds gather to listen.

schemes as PLUTO (the pipe line under the ocean which carried petrol under the English Channel to France) and 'FIDO', a method of dispersing fog from landing areas. Perhaps the most spectacular invention was the pre-fabricated Mulberry Harbour, which, when in position, floated up and down with the tide. The Mulberry Harbour was towed across to France and put in position after the D-Day landings to provide a dock for large ships to unload supplies.

D-Day ('D' standing for *Day*, the day when Europe would be attacked) successfully took place on 4th June 1944. Within a week Churchill visited the Normandy beaches where the forces had landed.

The end of the war was now in sight. Without delay, Churchill made many visits. He saw General Mont-

gomery in France, President Tito of Yugoslavia in Naples, President Roosevelt of the United States in Quebec, Joseph Stalin, the Russian dictator, in Moscow and General Charles de Gaulle, the French statesman, in liberated France.

From 4th to 11th February 1945, Churchill attended the Yalta Conference in the Crimea. Here he met President Roosevelt and Marshal Stalin. The three leaders discussed military operations and the conduct of the war, as well as the post war settlement of Europe.

They also arranged the date of 25th April for a Conference to be held in San Francisco, U.S.A. to prepare the Charter of a United Nations Organisation. The members of the United Nations Organisation would pledge themselves to the maintenance of international peace and security.

At Yalta, Churchill observed that Roosevelt, who suffered from polio, was far from well. Although Roosevelt attended to all matters of business with his usual efficiency, he was, in fact, very ill. He died two months later. Churchill had lost a personal friend and ally.

Eventually the fighting ceased. Churchill, as England's Prime Minister, had led the country to victory. He was not perfect and had made some mistakes and misjudgements, but he was always resolute in his purpose.

He never ceased to work for his ideals. He had prevented his country from being overrun by a tyrannical enemy, and his leadership in the war had helped to ensure the liberation of occupied Europe.

Germany finally surrendered unconditionally on VE (Victory in Europe) Day, 8th May 1945, and Japan was defeated three months later.

8 After the War

At the end of World War II, Churchill had reached the age of seventy. He was respected and revered by the whole nation. People knew how ably he had conducted the war and achieved victory and with what vigour he had stimulated and reassured the people.

But in peace-time, although his personal popularity remained very high, his political success began to diminish.

In July 1945, eleven weeks after hostilities ceased, a General Election was held. The Conservatives were defeated by the Labour party, who gained a majority of more than one hundred and fifty seats. Churchill

"The loyalties which centre upon Number One are enormous. If he trips, he must be sustained. If he makes mistakes, they must be covered. If he sleeps he must not be wantonly disturbed. If he is no good, he must be pole-axed."
Winston Churchill, Vol. 2 "Their Finest Hour".

Below Mr and Mrs Churchill drive through the crowds on their way to Churchill's installation as a Freeman of the City of London.

lost his parliamentary office as Prime Minister, but still remained a Member of Parliament, representing Woodford in Essex. He was succeeded as Prime Minister by Clement Attlee.

Several reasons for the Conservatives' massive defeat were put forward. Some said that Churchill in his election campaign was too aggressive — a policy ideal for war but not suitable for peace. Others thought the defeat was due to the Conservatives placing undue emphasis on the personality of Churchill rather than on a policy for re-building post-war Britain. Churchill was concerned that too much alteration might be made before the country had sufficiently recovered from the War to stand it.

Winston Churchill passed out of the limelight as Prime Minister. He was still, however, a Member of Parliament and the Leader of the Opposition and an active participant in world affairs.

Churchill received various honours at this time, including the award of the Order of Merit.

On 5th March 1946, an honorary degree was conferred on him at Westminster College, Fulton, Missouri, in the United States. The speech he made on this occasion was one of his most celebrated yet most provocative. While speaking of the continuing friendship between England and America, Churchill pointed out the dangers of Russian infiltration into other countries. He referred to the split which was occurring between East and West. He called it an 'Iron Curtain' which had descended across Europe.

Churchill's words eventually led to the formation of NATO, the North Atlantic Treaty Organisation. In the organisation the United States of America, Canada, and those European countries still free from Russian domination, united with each other for common defence.

Above This medal was awarded to Churchill by the American people, as a unique gesture to a man who was, after all the son of an American.

Opposite From an early age Churchill was rarely seen without a cigar. Many were gifts from admirers all over the world.

"A shadow had fallen upon the scenes so lately lighted by the Allied victory . . . From Stettin in the Baltic to Trieste in the Adriatic, an iron curtain has descended across the Continent. Behind that line lie all the capitals of the ancient states of Central and Eastern Europe . . . Warsaw, Berlin, Prague, Vienna, Budapest, Belgrade, Bucharest and Sofia . . ."
Winston Churchill, in his speech at Fulton, March 5th, 1946.

59

In September 1946, in a speech in Zurich, Switzerland, Winston Churchill pressed for a United States of Europe. This eventually resulted in the European Economic Community (EEC) and the Common Market.

Churchill now had more time for his personal activities. Two paintings he submitted to the Royal Academy were accepted for hanging in 1947. They were sent under the name of 'Mr. Winter' so that the famous name of Winston Churchill should not sway the judges in their choice. In April the following year, Churchill was made the first Royal Academician Extraordinary.

He undertook further writing activities. In addition to other works, he wrote the first volume of *The Second World War*, which was published in 1948. The complete work consisted of six volumes, the last of which was published in 1954.

Churchill concentrated on his political activities when the General Election of 1950 was fought. The Labour Government again won, but with a very small majority. Only eighteen months elapsed before another General Election was held.

This time the Conservatives were successful. Once again Churchill became Prime Minister and Minister of Defence. One month later he celebrated his seventy-seventh birthday.

He still travelled overseas, visiting Washington, Ottawa, Jamaica and Bermuda on parliamentary business.

King George VI was in failing health. When he died on 6th February 1952, it was Winston Churchill who counselled the young Queen Elizabeth II.

The following year the Knighthood of the Garter was conferred upon Churchill by the Queen and he became Sir Winston Churchill.

In October the same year he was awarded the Nobel Prize for Literature. These highly valued prizes are provided by money left by Alfred Nobel, a Swedish chemist and inventor. Nobel directed that annual prizes should be awarded for those benefiting humanity most in the fields of physics, chemistry, medicine, literature and the furtherance of peace in the world. Churchill's prize was the one awarded for literature.

Above Churchill on his way to Windsor to be installed as a Knight of the Garter.

"There is a great deal of difference between the tired man who wants a book to read and the alert man who wants to read a book."
Winston Churchill.

Above Churchill was awarded the Nobel Prize for Literature. This picture shows him working at a manuscript.

Opposite above To mark Churchill's 80th birthday, the House of Commons presented him with an illuminated book and a portrait by Graham Sutherland.

Opposite below In his later life Churchill was a popular figure and he could always be sure of a warm greeting from the crowds.

He gained it with his work *A History of the English Speaking Peoples*.

But Churchill was ageing. He suffered a stroke and his doctors advised him to rest. Even so, he held office for almost two more years before resigning as Prime Minister on 5th April 1955. He had celebrated his eightieth birthday almost six months earlier. He remained a Member of Parliament until finally leaving the House of Commons in the summer of 1964. Winston Churchill had served Parliament for over sixty-four years, and held every important Cabinet post except Foreign Secretary.

An honour which pleased Churchill immensely was conferred on him in 1963. He was made an honorary citizen of the United States of America. This was particularly appropriate, bearing in mind that his mother was American.

In 1964, one of Winston Churchill's last projects became a reality. As early as May 1958, Churchill realised that it was necessary for the country to increase the number of scientists and technologists. He foresaw that the nation must be ready for the Space Age.

With this in mind, Churchill launched an appeal to found a new college at Cambridge University. It was to be called 'Churchill College'. In 1964, the first section of the College was opened by the Duke of Edinburgh.

Churchill attained his 90th birthday on November 30th, 1964. He died on 24th January 1965. His strength had gradually declined during his last years but he had continued to enjoy life until a short while before his death.

Tributes came from many lands. Monarch and statesman, tradesman and workman, all mourned the passing of this great man. He had lived and served through six reigns.

Epilogue

Above Winston and Clementine Churchill. Their happy marriage and family life was a source of comfort to Churchill whenever his career seemed to be suffering a setback.

Winston Churchill became world famous in his lifetime. He was given a State funeral, which is normally an honour bestowed only on Royalty. Churchill requested that he should be buried in the village churchyard at Bladon, in Oxfordshire, where his parents and brother are buried. It is not far from Blenheim Palace, home of his ancestor, John Churchill, first Duke of Marlborough.

Winston Churchill enjoyed a happy family life. His wife always encouraged him in his endeavours and comforted him in his troubles. She undoubtedly played a great part in the success of his public and private activities. They celebrated their Golden Wedding (fifty years of marriage) in 1958.

Winston Churchill's main interest was his career, whether as a soldier, politician or writer. In more leisurely periods he turned to very different pursuits, usually practical activities such as painting pictures or bricklaying.

Churchill was fortunate to be healthy and strong. Apart from those infirmities he suffered when over the age of eighty, he had few serious illnesses. On three occasions he suffered from pneumonia. The first time was as a child. The other two attacks were in 1943 and 1944 during World War II. Each time Winston Churchill was back at his post within a short period.

He did, however, have quite a number of accidents. Some injuries were caused while engaged in sport, but others were caused by his own over enthusiasm or impetuosity.

Churchill became a familiar figure wherever he went. He wore such individual items of dress as a siren suit, a bow tie, or boots with zips, as suited the occasion. He was usually seen in public holding or smoking a cigar.

During World War II, his gruff voice was welcome as it came over the radio. His speeches contained many words of challenge, comfort and encouragement.

Throughout his life he always seemed to carry with him the words he wrote to his mother before he went into battle in the South African War: 'I shall believe I am to be preserved for future things'.

Churchill achieved fame as a war leader, politician, historian and writer. But underlying all this was a dedicated life of service to all mankind.

"Operation Hope Not".
The title Winston Churchill gave to his plans for his own funeral.

"He is history's child, and what he said and what he did will never die."
General de Gaulle, on the death of Churchill.

Below The Churchill most people will remember with his famous sign.

Principal Characters

Alexander, Field Marshal Harold (1891-1969). Commander in Chief Allied Armies in Italy in 1944 and Supreme Allied Commander Mediterranean Theatre, 1944-45.

Baldwin, Stanley (1867-1947). British Prime Minister, 1923-4, 1924-9 and 1935-7.

Chamberlain, Arthur Neville (1869-1940). British Prime Minister 1937-40. Signatory to the Munich Agreement.

Churchill, Lady Clementine Hozier (1885-1977). Wife of Sir Winston.

Churchill, Lady Jennie Jerome (1854-1922). Mother of Sir Winston Churchill.

Churchill, Lord Randolph (1849-1895). A notable politician and father of Sir Winston.

de Gaulle, Charles Andre Joseph Marie (1890-1970). French General and Statesman. Escaped after Dunkirk and organised Free French Movement. Became President of France in 1959.

Hitler, Adolf (1889-1945). German Dictator. Committed suicide.

Keynes, John Maynard (1883-1945). Noted British economist. His teachings had great influence.

Kitchener, General Sir Herbert (1850-1916). British Field Marshal. Took part in the Sudanese campaign, the South African War, and World War One.

Lloyd George, David (1863-1945). British Prime Minister, 1916-22.

Montgomery, Field Marshal Bernard Law (1887-1976). Commanded the 8th Army in Libya and won the Battle of El Alamein. Commanded Allied Armies on D-Day and took part in the liberation of North Europe.

Roosevelt, Franklin Delano (1882-1945). President of the United States of America.

Stalin, Joseph (1879-1953). Russian leader.

Table of Dates

1874   Birth of Winston Leonard Spencer Churchill.

1893   Churchill enters Sandhurst Military College.

1894-1900   Service with the Army.

1898   Publication of Churchill's first book — *The Malakand Field Force*.

1899   Churchill goes to South Africa as a Civilian War Correspondent, is taken prisoner and escapes.

1900   Churchill elected Member of Parliament for Oldham.

1904   Churchill leaves the Conservative Party and joins the Liberals.

1906   Churchill holds his first political office as Under Secretary of State for the Colonies.

1911   Churchill becomes First Lord of the Admiralty and strengthens the Navy.

1914-8   World War One.

1922   Churchill is defeated in the General Election.

1924   Churchill regains his Parliamentary Seat and re-joins the Conservative Party. He becomes the Chancellor of the Exchequer.

1926   The General Strike.

1938   The Munich Agreement.

1939-45   World War Two.

1940   Churchill becomes Prime Minister.

1945   Conservative defeat in the General Election. Churchill is succeeded as Prime Minister by Clement Attlee.

1946   The Fulton Speech in Missouri, U.S.A.

1948	Churchill made Royal Academician Extraordinary.
1951	Churchill again becomes Prime Minister.
1953	Churchill is Knighted. He is awarded the Nobel Prize for Literature.
1963	Churchill is made an honorary citizen of the U.S.A.
1964	Churchill College, Cambridge, opened by the Duke of Edinburgh.
1965	Death of Winston Leonard Spencer Churchill.

Picture Acknowledgements

Imperial War Museum 46, 47, 48, 50, 53, 54; National Army Museum 7; National Museum of Labour History 35; Popperfoto front cover; Radio Times Hulton Picture Library back cover, frontispiece, 6, 9, 11, 13, 14, 21, 23, 24, 25, 27, 28, 30, 31 (both), 32, 34, 37, 39, 40, 41, 42, 43, 44, 51, 52, 55, 57, 58, 59, 61, 62, 63 (both), 64, 65. Wayland Picture Library 8, 22, 26, 49.

Further reading

Briquebec, John *Winston Churchill* (Hart Davies 1972). A biography of Sir Winston written for children.

Chamberlin, E. R. *Life in Wartime Britain* (Batsford). An account of life during the war years.

Churchill, Winston *A History of the English Speaking Peoples* (Blenheim Edition, Cassell, 1965). Churchill's account of the development of the nation.

Dilkes, David *Sir Winston Churchill* (Hamish Hamilton 1965). A further study of Churchill's life.

Divine, David *The Nine Days of Dunkirk* (Pan). A record of the evacuation of the trapped army.

Frank, Anne *The Diary of Anne Frank* (Hutchinson, 1952). Entries in the diary of a Jewish girl living in hiding in Holland during the German occupation.

Hobbs, Anthony *The Battle of Britain* (Wayland, 1973). What happened when Britain fought alone.

Hobley, L. F. *The Second World War* (Ward Lock). An account of the outbreak and conduct of the war.

Liversidge, D. *Parliament — The Story of the Mother of Parliaments* (Franklin Watts, 1973). Information regarding Westminster.

Monham, Kathleen. *Growing Up in World War II* (Wayland 1979). The story of children' life during the Second World War.

Index